QUICK PASTA & NOODLE DISHES

IMP Limited

CONTENTS

Northern & Central Europe

New World

PASTA AND NOODLE DISHES FROM AROUND THE WORLD

Pasta dishes, whether classics from Italy or modern creations from the New World, are always a culinary delight and very quick and easy to prepare. From penne to spaghetti, pasta comes in an enormous variety of shapes and sizes and is now one of our favourite foods – whatever the occasion.

COOKING PASTA

The Italians, and all pasta lovers, are very careful not to cook their pasta for too long. Serving pasta 'al dente' means boiling it until the pasta is cooked through, but still slightly firm to the bite, not soggy. However, some people prefer their pasta firmer, some softer, so keep testing your pasta as you cook it until it is just as *you* like it. Drain the pasta in a colander by shaking gently. Don't shake it too hard or the pieces may stick together. Serve at once.

FRESH PASTA TIPS

Fresh pasta will keep for a couple of days in the fridge and must be eaten by the best-before date on the packet. If frozen on the day of purchase, it will keep for up to three months.

• Allow 25–50g/1–2oz more fresh pasta per person than dried. This is because dried pasta absorbs water when cooking and expands to become heavier.

• Fresh pasta cooks more quickly than dried. The time for both depends on the thickness of the pasta: some are ready in just one or two minutes.

• If using frozen pasta, there is no need to defrost it first, simply add it straight to the boiling water. Most shapes take the same time to cook as unfrozen pasta. If using frozen filled pasta, cook for an extra 4–5 minutes to ensure the filling is cooked through.

DRIED PASTA

Dried pasta is a versatile store cupboard essential and is now available in a wide range of shapes and colours. It will keep for up to four months, even after opening. When buying, check the best-before date on the packet.

WHAT SHAPE OF PASTA TO USE

Pasta shapes are designed to absorb and collect sauce. As a general rule shorter, fatter shapes are best served with richer, thick sauces and long thin varieties suit more delicate, light sauces.

These pastas are smooth and should be served with naturally clingy sauces, such as pesto.

Tagliatelle

Ravioli

Ravioli and tortellini are stuffed with a selection of herbs, vegetables, cheeses and/or meats. The sauce to accompany them should be light and delicate so that it complements the taste of the pasta and the filling rather than obscuring it.

Tortellini

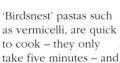

Paglia e fieno

Vermicelli

'Birdsnest' pastas such as vermicelli, are quick to cook – they only take five minutes – and should be served with a light, delicate sauce.

Penne

All these pastas are designed to collect sauce within their shape. They should be served with thick, hearty sauces.

Conchiglie

Orrechiette

Rotelli

Fusilli

ℱETTUCCINE IN FOUR CHEESE SAUCE

ITALY

Delicate fettuccine in a rich cheese sauce, with added cream, makes an easy but satisfying meal. Each contrasting cheese adds its own special flavour.

INGREDIENTS
(Serves 4)

- 400g/14oz fettuccine
- salt

FOR THE SAUCE
- 20g/¾oz butter
- 20g/¾oz plain flour
- 450ml/¾ pint milk
- salt and black pepper
- pinch of grated nutmeg
- 75g/3oz fontina or Gruyère cheese
- 75g/3oz Parmesan cheese
- 50g/2oz Gorgonzola cheese
- 50g/2oz mascarpone

INGREDIENTS TIP

For a stronger-flavoured sauce, substitute pecorino cheese for Parmesan. Pecorino is a pale yellow Italian cheese with a creamy texture. It is sold in varying strengths — the mature varieties have the stronger flavour.

1 For the sauce, melt the butter in a small saucepan. Stir in the flour and cook for a minute without letting the mixture brown.

2 Add the milk, a little at a time, stirring continuously. Season with salt, pepper and nutmeg. Bring to the boil and simmer for 2–3 minutes.

3 Meanwhile, cook the fettuccine in a large saucepan of salted, boiling water until al dente (follow packet instructions).

4 To make the sauce really smooth, pour it through a sieve into a new pan. Grate the fontina or Gruyère and the Parmesan cheeses. Crumble the Gorgonzola. Stir the mascarpone into the sauce until it is evenly combined, then add the other cheeses. Place the pan over a low heat and stir until the cheeses melt and the sauce is smooth.

5 Drain the fettuccine well in a large colander. Add the pasta to the cheese sauce and toss the mixture together until the pasta is evenly coated. Serve immediately.

Step 1

Step 2

Step 4

Preparation: **30** Min Cooking: **15** Min
Per Serving: 680 kcal/2865 kJ;
31g protein; 27g fat;
83g carbohydrate

TYPICALLY AOSTA VALLEY
One of the most famous cheeses of the region is fontina. It is produced on the mountain pastures during the summer months – just as it has been for centuries. Fontina has a mild, almost sweet aroma and is particularly good for cooking as it melts easily.

COOKING TIP

When stirring in the cheeses, keep the heat under the pan very low so they melt slowly into the sauce without becoming stringy • Freshly grated Parmesan cheese has a better flavour than the ready-grated version which can be dry and slightly stale tasting.

SERVING TIP

Garnish the pasta with fresh herbs and serve with a loaf of Italian bread, such as ciabatta or focaccia.

 A fresh, dry white wine such as Orvieto Classico, will provide a good foil for the rich cheese sauce.

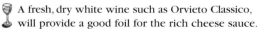

TAGLIERINI ALLA BOLOGNESE

ITALY

Sauce 'alla bolognese' is one of the mainstays of Italian cuisine. While it is served with spaghetti in most parts of the world, Italians prefer to eat it with the thinner taglierini.

INGREDIENTS
(Serves 4)

- 400g/14oz taglierini or spaghetti
- salt
- 40g/1½oz butter

FOR THE SAUCE

- 100g/4oz carrots
- 100g/4oz celery sticks
- 1 onion
- 1 clove garlic
- ½ bunch parsley
- 400g/14oz fresh tomatoes
- 1 tbsp olive oil
- 75g/3oz Parma ham
- 150g/5oz minced beef
- 150g/5oz minced pork
- 400g/14oz can plum tomatoes
- salt and black pepper
- 3 tbsp tomato purée
- 250ml/9fl oz chicken stock

INGREDIENTS TIP
Try adding a glass of red wine to the sauce in step 3.

1 Wash, trim and dice the carrots and celery. Peel the onion and garlic and chop finely. Wash and dry the parsley, then chop finely. Briefly stand the fresh tomatoes in boiling water, drain, then remove the skin and seeds. Dice the tomato flesh.

2 Heat the oil, add all the vegetables (except the tomatoes) and cook over a moderate heat for 5 minutes. Add the parsley and heat briefly. Dice the ham.

3 Add the minced meats and fry until evenly browned. Add the ham and cook for 5 minutes. Stir in the fresh tomatoes, then add the canned tomatoes, breaking them up with a spoon. Season and stir in the tomato purée. Add the stock, cover and cook over a medium heat for 45 minutes.

4 Meanwhile, cook the taglierini in a large saucepan of salted, boiling water until al dente (see packet instructions). Drain well.

5 Add the butter to the pasta and stir well. Divide between four warmed plates or dishes and spoon the sauce on top.

Step 1

Step 2

Step 3

Preparation: **20** Min Cooking: 1 hour
Per Serving: 810 kcal/3390 kJ;
38g protein; 34g fat;
84g carbohydrate

TYPICALLY EMILIA-ROMAGNA
The famous sauce 'alla bolognese' derives its name from Bologna, the capital of Emilia-Romagna. Even today, the locals take great delight in discussing at length which ingredients were used in the original recipe and which variations might be tolerated.

COOKING TIPS

Even the Italians vary their famous Bolognese sauce by adding different ingredients such as minced lamb or rabbit instead of beef and pork • A true Bolognese is simmered gently over a low heat for several hours and is less saucy than the version usually served.

SERVING TIP

A tomato, basil and mozzarella cheese salad (truly Italian in colour) makes an ideal starter for this meal.

 Serve a full-bodied Italian red wine with this dish, such as Sangiovese di Romagna or Chianti.

TAGLIATELLE IN SALMON SAUCE

ITALY

Pasta 'al salmone' is a true Italian classic. Tagliatelle, cooked al dente, perfectly complements the creamy sauce with its delicate pieces of salmon that melt in the mouth.

INGREDIENTS
(Serves 4)

- 400g/14oz tagliatelle
- salt
- a few fresh basil leaves, to garnish

FOR THE SAUCE

- 1 onion
- 40g/1½oz cold butter
- 125ml/4fl oz white wine
- 284ml/10fl oz double cream
- 350g/12oz fresh skinned salmon fillets
- salt and black pepper
- juice of ½ lime

INGREDIENTS TIP

Instead of fresh salmon you can use smoked salmon or salmon trout fillets. For a vegetarian dish, add 200g/7oz frozen peas to the cream sauce instead of the salmon.

1 Peel and finely chop the onion. Melt 15g/½oz butter in a pan. Add the onion and cook until softened but not browned. Add the wine and boil over a high heat for 2-3 minutes to reduce the liquid a little. Lower the heat, add the double cream and simmer until the sauce is reduced by half.

2 Meanwhile, cook the tagliatelle in a large saucepan of salted, boiling water until al dente (see packet instructions).

3 Cut the salmon fillets into 1 cm/½ inch cubes. Using an electric hand blender, purée the sauce in the saucepan. Add the remaining butter, stir well and season with salt, pepper and lime juice.

4 Add the salmon cubes to the sauce, cook for 5 minutes and remove from the heat. Drain the tagliatelle well and arrange on warmed serving plates.

5 Wash and dry the basil. Spoon the sauce over the pasta and sprinkle with basil leaves. Serve immediately.

Step 1

Step 3

Step 4

Preparation: **10** Min Cooking: 15 Min
Per Serving: 906 kcal/3784 kJ;
29g protein; 55g fat;
74g carbohydrate

TYPICALLY ITALIAN

Fish and seafood are an essential part of the menu in Italian restaurants. Side-dishes 'primi piatti' in particular often feature some kind of fish. And the trend is towards the so-called sophisticated pasta — pasta combined with exquisite fish and seafood.

COOKING TIP

Long, ribbon-like pasta such as fettuccine or wide pappardelle are also suitable for this recipe — the thick, creamy sauce sticks beautifully to the broad surface of the noodles. Combining the right shaped pasta with the right sauce in this way, means you aren't left with a lot of sauce in the dish after eating.

SERVING TIP

As a starter, serve a mushroom salad, 'insalata funghi' tossed in a vinaigrette dressing with herbs.

 A lively white wine such as a sparkling Spumante will complement the creamy salmon sauce.

SERVING TIP Serve the ravioli as a main course after a clear vegetable soup starter.

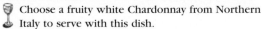 Choose a fruity white Chardonnay from Northern Italy to serve with this dish.

12

RAVIOLI IN PARSLEY SAUCE

ITALY

Fresh ravioli is particularly tasty served in this aromatic parsley sauce. Using white wine and cream in the sauce turns a popular dish into a really special meal.

INGREDIENTS
(Serves 4)

- 800g/1¾lb fresh ravioli with meat filling
- salt

FOR THE SAUCE

- 1 onion
- 1 clove garlic
- 40g/1½oz butter
- 15g/½oz plain flour
- 125ml/4fl oz white wine
- 125ml/4fl oz milk
- 300ml/½ pint double cream
- 1 bunch flat-leaved parsley
- salt and white pepper
- pinch of cayenne pepper
- 1 tsp lemon juice

INGREDIENTS TIP

Depending on the season, chives or a few sprigs of thyme are a good substitute for parsley. Look in the chiller cabinet of major supermarkets for fresh ravioli.

1 For the ravioli, bring a large saucepan of salted water to the boil. Add the ravioli and cook in the simmering water until tender (see packet instructions). Drain the ravioli. Meanwhile, peel and finely chop the onion and garlic for the sauce.

2 Heat the butter in a small saucepan, add the chopped onion and garlic and cook until softened but do not allow to brown. Sprinkle in the flour and cook briefly, stirring constantly, then add the wine. Continue stirring the mixture to blend the wine with the sauce.

3 Pour in the milk and the double cream. Bring the sauce back to the boil, then reduce the heat and simmer for 10 minutes.

4 Wash and dry the parsley, chop coarsely and stir into the sauce. Reheat briefly, then remove the pan from the heat. Season with salt, pepper, cayenne pepper and lemon juice to taste.

5 Arrange the drained ravioli on warmed serving plates. Pour the parsley sauce over the pasta and serve hot.

Step 1

Step 2

Step 4

Preparation: **15** Min Cooking: 20 Min
Per Serving: 574 kcal/2380 kJ;
7g protein; 50g fat;
21g carbohydrate

TYPICALLY LIGURIAN

The coast of the province of Liguria in northern Italy is steep and rugged and does not lend itself to cattle-breeding or cultivating vegetables. That is why the Ligurian cuisine is fairly basic and often vegetarian. Its main appeal is the abundant use of fresh herbs.

ℙAPPARDELLE WITH MUSHROOMS

ITALY

The extra wide ribbons forms an ideal basis for the sauce which combines the delicate, slightly nutty flavour of mushrooms with juicy tomatoes and aromatic fresh herbs.

INGREDIENTS
(Serves 4)

- 400g/14oz pappardelle or tagliatelle
- salt
- knob of butter
- grated Parmesan cheese

FOR THE SAUCE

- 40g/1½oz dried porcini mushrooms
- 350g/12oz fresh tomatoes
- 1 sprig thyme
- basil and parsley leaves
- 1 onion
- 1 clove garlic
- 4 tbsp olive oil
- 100g/4oz celery
- salt and black pepper

INGREDIENTS TIP

Dried Italian porcini are available from delicatessens and large supermarkets. Use 250g/9oz sliced chestnut mushrooms if you prefer and omit step 1 of the recipe.

1 Place the porcini in a bowl and pour over boiling water to cover. Leave to stand for 30 minutes then drain — the soaking water can be used as stock for another recipe.

2 Cook the pappardelle or tagliatelle in a large saucepan of salted, boiling water until al dente (see packet instructions).

3 Meanwhile, briefly stand the tomatoes in boiling water, drain and remove the skin. Cut into quarters, remove seeds and chop the flesh. Wash and dry the herbs. Chop the onion and garlic.

4 Heat the oil in a frying pan, add the chopped onion and garlic and cook until softened but not brown. Chop the celery, add to the pan and cook for 1–2 minutes. Increase the heat, add the porcini and cook for 2–3 minutes, stirring frequently. Season with salt and pepper. Add the tomatoes and herbs and cook for 1–2 minutes.

5 Drain the pasta and toss with the butter. Arrange on individual plates. Spoon the mushroom and vegetable mixture over the pasta and serve immediately with the grated Parmesan cheese.

Step 1

Step 4

Step 5

Preparation: **35** Min Cooking: **10** Min
Per Serving: 510 kcal/2152 kJ;
14g protein; 17g fat;
79g carbohydrate

TYPICALLY PIEDMONT

The morning mists in the forests of Piedmont herald the arrival of the mushroom season. The most popular and most widely available Italian wild mushrooms are porcini or ceps. They are used fresh or dried in many recipes including soups, sauces, stuffings and risottos and pasta dishes like this.

COOKING TIP

Dried mushrooms need to be soaked in boiling water for at least 30 minutes before they can be added to a dish. Soaking makes them swell to several times their size so less are needed than fresh. The soaking water makes a delicious rich stock which can be used to add a strong mushroom flavour to soups and sauces.

SERVING TIP

Vanilla ice-cream mixed with blueberries and topped with whipped cream makes an excellent choice of dessert to follow this luxurious dish.

 A full-bodied red wine from Piedmont, such as Barbaresco, complements the mushroom flavour.

S E R V I N G   T I P   Warm ciabatta bread rolls make an
excellent accompaniment to the pasta.

 A dry white wine, such as Frascati, would go very
well with this dish.

$\mathscr{P}$ENNE IN SPICY SAUCE

ITALY

The traditional name for this dish is 'all'arrabbiata' meaning 'in a hot manner'. Its few, yet perfectly harmonising, ingredients combine to create a fiery, piquant mix of flavours.

INGREDIENTS
(Serves 4)

- 400g/14oz penne
- salt
- ½ bunch flat-leaved parsley, to garnish

FOR THE SAUCE
- 100g/4oz smoked streaky bacon
- 500g/1lb 2oz fresh tomatoes
- 2 cloves garlic
- 1 onion
- 2 red chillies
- 1 tbsp olive oil
- salt and white pepper

INGREDIENTS TIP

Instead of peeling and sieving fresh tomatoes, substitute 300g/10oz of tomato passata, thick tomato pasta sauce or chopped tinned tomatoes.

1 Cut the rind off the bacon and dice finely. Briefly stand the tomatoes in boiling water, drain, rinse in cold water and remove the skin. Cut the tomatoes into quarters, remove the seeds, dice the tomato flesh and press through a sieve.

2 Cook the penne in a large saucepan of salted, boiling water until al dente (see packet instructions).

3 Peel the garlic and onion and chop finely. Cut the chillies in half lengthwise, remove seeds and membrane and finely chop the flesh. Wash your hands thoroughly.

4 Heat the oil in a frying-pan and fry the bacon gently until the fat begins to run. Add the chopped garlic and onion and cook until softened. Add the sieved tomatoes and the chillies. Lower the heat and simmer until the sauce is slightly reduced. Season generously with salt and pepper.

5 Drain the penne well and return to the saucepan. Wash and dry the parsley, then chop coarsely. Add the sauce and parsley to the penne and toss together until combined.

Step 1

Step 3

Step 5

Preparation: **20** Min Cooking: **20** Min
Per Serving: 571 kcal/2410 kJ;
22g protein; 29g fat;
79g carbohydrate

TYPICALLY LAZIO
While Rome is a cosmopolitan city, life in the surrounding Lazio countryside is much more sedate and this is reflected in the simple local cuisine. Meat is cooked only once or twice a week, but the local fresh fruit and vegetables are used to create mouth-watering dishes.

LINGUINE WITH RICOTTA AND HERBS

ITALY

A light meal quickly prepared. The subtle contrast between the sweet tomato sauce and the sharper taste of the ricotta cheese is the secret of its success.

INGREDIENTS
(Serves 4)

- 400g/14oz linguine or another long thin pasta
- salt

FOR THE SAUCE

- 50g/2oz fresh herbs (e.g. parsley, chervil, sage, thyme, rosemary, tarragon or basil)
- 2 onions
- 10 to 12 small tomatoes
- 6 tbsp olive oil
- salt and white pepper
- 200g/7oz ricotta cheese

INGREDIENTS TIP

If you cannot find ricotta cheese, any cream cheese will do. Choose herbs that are in season and readily available and use them as fresh as possible so they retain all their flavour.

1 For the sauce, wash and dry the herbs and coarsely chop with a sharp knife. Peel the onions and chop finely. Wash the tomatoes and cut into quarters.

2 Heat the olive oil in a shallow saucepan. Add the onions and cook until softened but not browned.

Step 2

3 Add the tomatoes, cook briefly and season with salt and pepper. Simmer for a few minutes until the tomatoes soften.

4 Meanwhile, cook the linguine in a large saucepan of salted, boiling water until al dente (see packet instructions). Drain well.

Step 3

5 Add the chopped herbs to the sauce and stir well to let the flavours develop. Add some more seasoning, if desired.

6 Toss the pasta with the sauce in the saucepan until well combined. Remove the pan from the heat, break up the ricotta cheese with a fork and toss with the pasta and sauce. Serve immediately.

Step 6

Preparation: **15** Min Cooking: **15** Min
Per Serving: 674 kcal/2827 kJ;
18g protein; 33g fat;
81g carbohydrate

TYPICALLY SARDINIAN

The Italian soft cheese, ricotta, is made from the whey left over when producing other cheeses. Different types of milk are used depending on the region. In northern Italy, it is produced from cow's milk, whereas the Sardinians traditionally use sheep's milk.

COOKING TIPS

Removing the saucepan from the heat before mixing the ricotta into the pasta ensures that the cheese retains its creamy texture • This dish can be reheated the following day — just add a little olive oil to keep it moist and to stop the pasta sticking together.

SERVING TIP

An 'insalata mista' – mixed salad – makes an ideal starter. Serve an Italian white bread with the main course.

Serve Verdiccio, a fruity Italian white wine, which goes well with this dish.

CREAMY FLORENTINE TAGLIATELLE

ITALY

Serve this tender spinach and smooth cream sauce with popular Italian ribbon pasta for a vegetarian feast. Parmesan cheese and lemon juice add an authentic flavour.

INGREDIENTS
(Serves 4)

- 400g/14oz tagliatelle
- salt

FOR THE SAUCE

- 500g/1lb 2oz fresh spinach
- 1 onion
- 1 clove garlic
- 20g/¾oz butter
- salt and white pepper
- pinch of nutmeg
- 200ml/7fl oz double cream
- 50g/2oz grated Parmesan
- 1 tbsp lemon juice

INGREDIENTS TIP

Tender young spinach with its light green leaves and mild taste is ideal for this dish. In late summer and winter, use the stronger and fuller flavoured winter spinach, or frozen chopped spinach.

1 For the sauce, trim the spinach, pull away any coarse ribs and discard any yellow leaves. If using baby spinach, the tender stems can be used. Rinse the leaves well in several changes of cold water until the water is free of any dirt or grit. Drain well. Peel and chop the onion and garlic.

Step 1

2 Melt the butter in a large saucepan and cook the onion and garlic until softened but not browned. Add the spinach and cook for 2–3 minutes, stirring constantly. Season generously with salt, pepper and nutmeg.

3 Pour in the cream, lower the heat and cook gently, stirring constantly, until the sauce reduces a little.

Step 3

4 Meanwhile, cook the tagliatelle in a large saucepan of salted, boiling water until al dente (see packet instructions). Drain well.

5 Add the Parmesan to the sauce and stir well. Add the lemon juice and then toss the pasta with the sauce and serve hot, sprinkled with extra cheese.

Step 5

Preparation: **15** Min Cooking: 15 Min
Per Serving: 674 kcal/2824 kJ;
21g protein; 34g fat;
76g carbohydrate

TYPICALLY TUSCAN

Like all Italians, Tuscans enjoy diversity when it comes to pasta. As a result, their pasta comes in all shapes and colours – spinach, saffron, beetroot juice as well as the ink of squid are used to produce a variety of coloured pastas and enhance the taste of the dough.

COOKING TIP

If using mature spinach with large leaves rather than fresh baby spinach, you should cut away any coarse stalks and shred the leaves before cooking. Large leaves tend to clump together and you may find them difficult to separate when stirred into the sauce.

SERVING TIP

As a starter, serve a radicchio salad with rings of white or red onion in a classic vinaigrette dressing.

 Serve a dry white wine from Tuscany, such as Frascati, with the meal.

SERVING TIP Lemon slices and marinated, stoned olives make an attractive side dish.

A robust Sicilian red wine such as Corvo would go well with this dish.

ℱETTUCCINE WITH MEATBALLS

ITALY

Fresh sage, garlic and lemon add the Sicilian touch to this hearty dish, while the meatballs and Parmesan cheese provide the Mediterranean flavours.

INGREDIENTS
(Serves 4)

- 400g/14oz fettuccine
- salt

FOR THE MEATBALLS
- 1 large stale bread roll
- 125ml/4fl oz tepid milk
- 2 slices cooked ham
- 200g/7oz minced beef
- 200g/7oz minced pork
- 2 tbsp grated Parmesan
- 2 eggs, 1 egg yolk
- salt and black pepper
- pinch of cayenne pepper
- 3 tbsp olive oil

FOR THE GARNISH
- 1 clove garlic
- a few fresh sage leaves
- 4 tbsp olive oil
- juice of ½ lemon

INGREDIENTS TIP
Try substituting oregano or basil, available fresh in supermarkets, for the sage.

1 For the meatballs, slice the bread roll and soak in the milk. Dice the ham and place in a large bowl with the minced meats.

2 Squeeze the bread roll and add to the meats. Add the Parmesan, eggs, egg yolk, salt, black pepper and cayenne and stir until well mixed. Shape into small balls.

3 Heat the oil in a frying pan and fry the meatballs for about 10 minutes until browned. Drain, set aside and keep warm.

4 Cook the fettuccine in a large saucepan of salted, boiling water until al dente (see packet instructions). Peel and finely chop the garlic. Wash, dry and coarsely chop the sage leaves.

5 Heat the olive oil in a frying pan. Add the garlic, sage and the meatballs and cook for 1–2 minutes, stirring continuously. Add the lemon juice.

6 Drain the fettuccine well and arrange in individual soup bowls. Spoon the meatballs and sage leaves on top and serve.

Step 1

Step 2

Step 3

Preparation: **20 Min** Cooking: **20 Min**
Per Serving: 920 kcal/3854 kJ;
42g protein; 50g fat;
82g carbohydrate

TYPICALLY SICILIAN
A Sicilian menu reflects the changeable history of the country and the different ingredients introduced over the centuries. The Arabs brought citrus fruit to this fertile island and the Sicilians often use lemon and sage with roast meat.

FETTUCCINE WITH PESTO

ITALY

Flat ribbon pasta tossed with the famous basil, garlic and cheese sauce makes a classic Italian dish that's deliciously simple but distinctively flavoured.

INGREDIENTS
(Serves 4)

- 400g/14oz fettuccine
- salt

FOR THE SAUCE

- 2 cloves garlic
- 75g/3oz pine nuts
- ¼ tsp salt
- 50g/2oz fresh basil
- 90g/3½oz grated Parmesan
- 25g/1oz grated pecorino
- 175ml/6fl oz olive oil

INGREDIENTS TIP

Apart from the basil, pine nuts and olive oil, the cheeses determine the distinctive flavour of pesto sauce. Try out some of the different types and brands of pesto, available in delicatessens and supermarkets, to find the variety you enjoy the most.

1 For the sauce, peel the garlic. Place the garlic, pine nuts and salt in a mortar and pound with a pestle until finely ground. Alternatively, purée in a food processor.

Step 1

2 Wash and dry the basil, tear the leaves off the stems and cut into strips. Gradually add to the mortar and gently pound, or purée, with the garlic mixture.

3 Gradually add the finely grated Parmesan and pecorino cheeses and mix well. Add the olive oil, first drop by drop, then a little faster, stirring continuously, until the paste becomes thick and creamy. Cover the sauce and store in a cool place.

Step 3

4 Cook the fettuccine in a large saucepan of salted, boiling water until al dente (see packet instructions). Drain well.

5 Place the pasta in a large, warmed mixing bowl and add the pesto. Using 2 tablespoons, toss the pasta in the sauce until well coated. Arrange the pasta on warmed plates and serve immediately.

Step 5

Preparation: **35** Min Cooking: 10 Min
Per Serving: 1021 kcal/4259 kJ;
21g protein; 69g fat;
84g carbohydrate

TYPICALLY LIGURIAN

The classic pesto from Genoa is prepared differently in other Mediterranean regions or countries. Some regions make pesto with walnuts instead of pine nuts, while others substitute basil with parsley. Diced tomatoes are also added to some pesto sauces.

COOKING TIP

Basil develops its full aroma in summer so if you're a fan of pesto this is the time to stock up. Prepare the sauce following the recipe and freeze in small portions. To store in the fridge, pour the pesto into a jar and cover with a little olive oil – it will keep for about two weeks.

SERVING TIP

The perfect dessert to follow this dish is Tiramisù, the classic Italian mascarpone cheese and coffee trifle.

🍷 Serve a fruity white wine with this dish, such as the Australian Jacob's Creek Chardonnay.

FUSILLI WITH TUNA AND TOMATOES

ITALY

This colourful and easy recipe with its tangy sauce of tuna, herbs and tomatoes, combines many of the Mediterranean's most popular flavours.

INGREDIENTS
(Serves 4)

- 400g/14oz fusilli
- salt and black pepper
- basil leaves, to garnish

FOR THE SAUCE

- 4 shallots
- 1 tbsp olive oil
- 400g/14oz can tomatoes
- 4 sun-dried tomatoes
- 2 x 200g/7oz cans tuna
- 1 tbsp chopped fresh marjoram or oregano
- 75g/3oz stoned black olives, optional

INGREDIENTS TIP

Jars or packets of sun-dried tomatoes are available from delicatessens and larger supermarkets. They have quite a salty flavour so don't add extra salt to the sauce without tasting first.

1 Peel and finely slice the shallots. Heat the oil in a frying pan, add the shallots and fry gently for about 5 minutes until softened. Stir in the canned tomatoes and simmer for 10 minutes, or until the sauce reduces and thickens slightly.

2 While the tomato sauce is simmering, cook the fusilli in a large pan of boiling, salted water until al dente (follow packet instructions).

3 Cut the sun-dried tomatoes into thin strips. Drain the tuna and flake into chunks. Stir the tuna and the sun-dried tomatoes into the tomato sauce and simmer for a further 5 minutes.

4 Add the marjoram or oregano and olives, if using, to the tuna and tomato sauce. Season to taste with salt and black pepper.

5 Drain the pasta and serve with the sauce spooned over. Scatter the dish with a few basil leaves.

Step 1

Step 3

Step 3

Preparation: **15** Min Cooking: **20** Min
Per Serving: 537 kcal/2270 kJ;
34g protein; 17g fat;
66g carbohydrate

TYPICALLY ITALIAN

Fish sauces for pasta are popular in southern Italy, particularly Sicily where fresh tuna is a familiar sight in the markets. Bluefin tuna is the most expensive and most sought-after variety, and many of the best cuts will be bought by Japanese sushi merchants.

SERVING TIP Smaller portions of this dish make perfect starters — this amount of pasta will serve six.

 A dry Italian white wine such as Orvieto or Frascati is perfect with this meal.

GREEK MACARONI SUNSHINE BAKE

GREECE

Tasty mince, macaroni and a creamy yoghurt and cheese sauce are layered together in this traditional oven-baked dish from Greece called Pastitsio.

INGREDIENTS
(Serves 4)

- 1 onion
- 2 tbsp vegetable oil
- 450g/1lb minced lamb
- 400g/14oz can chopped tomatoes
- 2 tbsp tomato purée
- salt and black pepper
- 150ml/¼ pint lamb stock
- 1 tsp dried mixed herbs
- 225g/8oz macaroni
- 500g/1lb 2oz Greek yoghurt
- 1 tbsp cornflour
- 2 eggs
- 6 tbsp halloumi or Parmesan cheese, grated
- 1 tbsp chopped fresh oregano or 1 tsp dried

INGREDIENTS TIP

Halloumi is a semi-hard cheese made from goats' milk. It has a mild flavour and a slightly rubbery texture. If you can't find it, use Parmesan instead.

1 Finely slice the onion. Heat the oil in a large frying pan and fry the onion until softened. Add the minced lamb and fry over a medium heat until the meat turns pale and starts to brown.

2 Add the tomatoes, tomato purée, seasoning, stock and herbs and bring to the boil. Lower the heat and simmer for 25–30 minutes, stirring occasionally, until the excess liquid has evaporated and the sauce becomes quite thick.

3 Meanwhile, cook the macaroni until al dente (follow packet instructions). Spoon the meat mixture into a shallow ovenproof dish. Preheat the oven to 180°C/350°F/Gas 4.

4 Beat together the yoghurt, cornflour, eggs, 3 tablespoons of cheese and the oregano. Mix a third of this mixture with the pasta and pour onto the meat.

5 Spoon the rest of the yoghurt mixture on top and sprinkle over the remaining cheese. Bake for 25–30 minutes, or until golden and bubbling. Serve immediately.

Step 1

Step 3

Step 5

Preparation: **30 Min**
Cooking: **1¼ Hours**
Per Serving: 700 kcal/2935 kJ;
34 g protein; 46 g fat;
40 g carbohydrate

TYPICALLY GREEK

The dry, rugged Greek terrain is good for grazing sheep, so lamb is used in many traditional dishes such as Moussaka, Souvlakia and Kleftiko. Many herbs also grow wild, particularly oregano and thyme which are used widely in Greek cooking.

SERVING TIP A salad of tomatoes, cucumber, olives, onions and feta makes a refreshing first course.

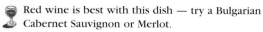 Red wine is best with this dish — try a Bulgarian Cabernet Sauvignon or Merlot.

GREEK-STYLE RIGATONI WITH COURGETTES

GREECE

Lightly fried courgettes cooked in an onion and cream sauce are complemented by the fresh taste of feta cheese. Serve sprinkled with basil for a quick and delicious meal.

INGREDIENTS
(SERVES 4)

- 400g/14oz rigatoni
- salt

FOR THE SAUCE

- 575g/1¼lb small courgettes
- 2 tbsp olive oil
- 1 onion
- 100g/4oz smoked streaky bacon
- salt and pepper
- 125ml/4fl oz double cream
- 200g/7oz feta cheese
- a few basil leaves

INGREDIENTS TIP

Peel and crush a clove of garlic and fry it with the onion to give the dish a more pungent flavour. Garlic burns easily, so fry over a gentle heat to stop it going too brown and tasting bitter.

1 Using a vegetable peeler, remove thin strips of skin from the courgettes to create a striped pattern. Cut the courgettes in half lengthways and scrape out the seeds with a teaspoon.

2 Slice the courgettes into 6mm/¾in chunks. Heat the oil in a large frying pan. Peel and chop the onion and fry until slightly golden. Finely chop the bacon, add to the pan and fry briefly tossing all the time. Add the diced courgettes and season with salt and pepper. Pour in the cream and simmer gently for 6–8 minutes.

3 Cook the rigatoni in a large saucepan of salted, boiling water until al dente (follow packet instructions).

4 Crumble the feta cheese into a large mixing bowl. Wash and dry the basil and shred the leaves with a sharp knife. Drain the pasta thoroughly in a large colander and toss with the feta cheese.

5 Stir the pasta into the courgette mixture and toss to coat. Sprinkle with the basil leaves and serve immediately.

Step 1

Step 2

Step 2

Preparation: **45** Min Cooking: **15** Min
Per Serving: 570 kcal/3221 kJ;
25g protein; 43g fat;
76g carbohydrate

TYPICALLY GREEK

The Greeks' favourite variety of cheese is feta – which translates as 'piece'. Traditionally, feta is made from sheeps' milk, but today is more likely to be made from cows' milk. Feta is stored in brine, which makes it harder and gives it its distinctive salty taste.

COOKING TIP

Simmering the cream in the sauce allows some of the
liquid in the cream to evaporate and the sauce to
thicken a little. Double cream has a high fat content
and can be heated to a higher temperature than
single cream which has a lower fat content and will
separate or curdle when boiled.

SERVING TIP

Finish the meal with a serving of
traditional Greek baklava, made from filo
pastry, honey and walnuts.

Serve with a chilled Demestica wine followed by a
measure of Greek ouzo after the baklava.

ᴀNDALUSIAN PASTA SOUP

SPAIN

Pasta soups, such as Italian minestrone, are usually a meal in themselves and this Spanish speciality is no exception. Spicy chorizo sausages add the warmth of chilli to the tomato base.

INGREDIENTS
(Serves 4)

- 1 large Spanish onion
- 2 cloves garlic
- 1 red pepper
- 2 celery sticks
- 225g/8oz chorizo sausages
- 2 tbsp olive oil
- 600ml/1 pint vegetable stock
- 300ml/½ pint tomato pasta sauce
- 400g/14oz can flageolet beans
- 100g/4oz soup pasta
- salt and black pepper

TO GARNISH
- flat-leaved parsley
- grated Parmesan cheese

INGREDIENTS TIP

Soup pastas are tiny star or shell shapes that cook quickly when added to a hot liquid. They add extra texture and body to a soup.

1 Peel and finely chop the onion and peel and chop the garlic cloves into fine slivers. Halve the pepper, remove the seeds, stalk and the white pith and chop the flesh into 1cm/½in chunks. Slice the celery into small pieces and cut the sausages into bite-sized chunks.

2 Heat the oil in a large saucepan and fry the onion gently until softened but not browned. Add the chopped garlic, pepper, celery and sausages and fry for 5 minutes, stirring frequently.

3 Pour the stock and pasta sauce into the saucepan. Cook over a medium heat until the mixture starts to simmer.

4 Drain the beans and add, with the pasta, to the soup. Lower the heat and simmer gently for 15 minutes with the pan uncovered, so the soup thickens a little.

5 Season to taste with salt and pepper and ladle into deep soup bowls. Garnish with parsley sprigs and serve with grated Parmesan on the table to sprinkle on top.

Step 1

Step 2

Step 3

Preparation: **20 Min** Cooking: **25 Min**

Per Serving: 399 kcal/1675 kJ;
17g protein; 19g fat;
44g carbohydrate

TYPICALLY SPANISH

Chorizo sausages are made of pork and pimiento — a red chilli pepper — and have a warm, spicy flavour. They are very popular in Spain and are often added to casseroles and paella dishes. Other flavoured sausages can also be used for this recipe.

SERVING TIP Warmed garlic and herb bread
tastes delicious with this soup.

Try a warm, full-bodied Spanish red wine such as
a Rioja or Valencia.

SERVING TIP Serve as a starter for six, in individual ovenproof dishes topped with Gruyère.

 Serve a chilled, dry French white wine or Provençal rosé during the summer months.

PASTA SHELLS WITH ROASTED VEGETABLES

FRANCE

Richly coloured Mediterranean vegetables are oven-roasted with olive oil, garlic and aromatic herbs to make a vivid sauce for pasta shells. A sprinkling of cheese adds the finishing touch.

INGREDIENTS
(Serves 4)

- 400g/14oz pasta shells

FOR THE SAUCE

- 1 aubergine
- 1 courgette
- 1 red, 1 yellow and 1 green pepper
- 4 shallots
- 6 large tomatoes
- 3 garlic cloves
- 6 tbsp olive oil
- 2 tsp dried herbes de Provence
- ground black pepper
- salt
- grated Parmesan or Gruyère cheese, to serve

INGREDIENTS TIP

Other short pasta shapes can be substituted for the shells such as farfalle, or bow ties. Tossing the cooked pasta with olive oil keeps the pieces separate and adds flavour.

1 Preheat the oven to 200°C/400°F/Gas 6. Trim the stalk from the aubergine and the courgette and cut into small chunks. Halve the peppers, remove the seeds and white pith and cut into pieces about the same size as the aubergine and courgette chunks.

2 Peel the shallots and cut into quarters. Cut the tomatoes into wedges and peel and slice the garlic. Spread the vegetables in a very large, shallow roasting tin.

3 Drizzle the vegetables with 4 tablespoons of olive oil and sprinkle with the herbs and pepper. Roast the vegetables for 30 minutes, turning them once or twice during cooking.

4 When the vegetables have been cooking for about 20 minutes, cook the pasta in a large pan of boiling, salted water until al dente (follow packet instructions).

5 Drain the pasta, toss with the remaining olive oil and serve with the vegetables, spooning over any juices from the roasting tin. Serve with grated Parmesan or Gruyère cheese sprinkled on top.

Step 1

Step 2

Step 3

Preparation: **20** Min Cooking: **30** Min
Per Serving: 530 kcal/2233 kJ;
13g protein; 24g fat;
71g carbohydrate

TYPICALLY PROVENÇAL

During the summer the warm Mediterranean sun ripens locally grown vegetables, giving them a wonderfully sweet flavour. This recipe, which uses a variety of fresh vegetables, is a variation on traditional ratatouille – the vegetables are oven-roasted rather than stewed.

3 WAYS WITH TOMATO PASTA SAUCE

For a successful sauce, the tomatoes have to be of the best quality. Here are three aromatic variations from different regions of Italy.

SPAGHETTI IN PIQUANT TOMATO SAUCE

Preparation: **10** Min Cooking: **20** Min

CALABRIA

(SERVES 4)
- 400g/14oz spaghetti
- salt

FOR THE SAUCE
- 1kg/2¼lb ripe tomatoes
- 1 onion
- 2-3 cloves garlic
- 2 tbsp olive oil
- 1 red chilli
- 125ml/4fl oz red wine
- salt and black pepper

1 Remove the stalks from the tomatoes and briefly stand the tomatoes in boiling water. Rinse with cold water and remove the skin. Cut into quarters, remove seeds and dice.

2 Peel the onion and garlic cloves and chop finely.

3 Heat the oil in a frying pan, add the onion and garlic and the whole chilli. Cook until the onions are soft but not brown.

4 Add the tomatoes and the wine. Season with salt and pepper and cook until the sauce thickens.

5 Cook the spaghetti in a large saucepan of salted, boiling water until al dente (see packet instructions), then drain well. Arrange on individual plates. Remove the chilli from the sauce and pour over the spaghetti.

SPAGHETTI I SAUC

Preparation: **10** M

SICILY

(SERVES 4)
- 400g/14oz spaghetti
- salt

FOR THE SAUCE
- 1kg/2¼lb ripe tomatoes
- 100g/4oz butter
- salt and black pepper
- a few basil leaves

1 Cook the spaghetti in plenty of salted, boiling water until al dente (follow packet instructions).

2 Meanwhile, remove stalks from the tomatoes, briefly stand in boiling water, rinse

SPAGHETTI IN CREAMY TOMATO SAUCE

Preparation: **15** Min Cooking: **25** Min

EMILIA-ROMAGNA

(SERVES 4)
- 400g/14oz spaghetti
- salt

FOR THE SAUCE
- 800g1/¾lb ripe tomatoes
- 60g/2½oz smoked bacon
- 1 onion
- 1 tbsp olive oil
- salt and black pepper
- 4-5 tbsp whipping cream

1 Wash the tomatoes and cut into quarters. Remove seeds and dice the flesh.

2 Dice the bacon. Peel the onion and chop finely.

3 Heat the oil in a saucepan and fry the bacon gently until the fat begins to run. Add the onion and cook until softened but not browned. Add the tomatoes and season with salt and pepper. Cover and cook over a moderate heat for 15–20 minutes.

4 Meanwhile, cook the spaghetti in plenty of salted, boiling water until al dente (see packet instructions). Drain well and arrange on individual plates.

5 Using an electric hand blender, coarsely purée the sauce, then reheat. Stir in the cream and season to taste.

FRESH TOMATO WITH BASIL

ooking: **10** Min

with cold water and remove the skin. Cut the tomatoes into quarters, remove the seeds and dice the flesh.

3 Melt the butter in a medium saucepan, add the tomatoes and simmer for a few minutes.

4 Season the sauce generously with salt and pepper. Shred the basil leaves into fine slivers and stir into the sauce.

5 Drain the pasta well and arrange on individual plates. Add the sauce, toss with the spaghetti, garnish with torn basil leaves and serve immediately.

HUNGARIAN PASTA WITH PAPRIKA

HUNGARY

INGREDIENTS
(Serves 4)

- 400g/14oz macaroni
- salt
- knob of butter
- 1 tbsp chopped fresh parsley

FOR THE SAUCE

- 1 red, 1 yellow and 1 green pepper
- 1 onion
- 2 cloves garlic
- 3 tbsp olive oil
- 1 sprig thyme
- 1 bay leaf
- 1 tsp hot paprika powder
- pinch of caraway seeds
- 250ml/9fl oz stock
- salt and black pepper

INGREDIENTS TIP

For a milder flavour, use ordinary paprika rather than the hot variety.

A vibrant and colourful way to brighten up pasta. The piquant sauce uses Hungary's favourite spice, hot paprika, which gives the lightly buttered, curly pasta a real flavour boost.

1 For the sauce, cut the peppers in half, remove the seeds and place on a baking tray, skin-side up. Roast in the oven at the highest temperature, or grill, until the skin blisters and chars.

2 Meanwhile, peel the onion and garlic and slice thinly. Remove peppers from the oven or grill. Cover with a damp cloth and then remove the skin. Dice the flesh.

3 Cook the pasta in a large saucepan of salted, boiling water until al dente (see packet instructions). Drain well.

4 Heat the olive oil in a saucepan, add the onion and garlic and cook until softened but not browned. Add the thyme, bay leaf, paprika powder and caraway seeds and stir well. Add the diced peppers. Reduce the heat and add the stock. Cover and simmer for 10 minutes. Season with salt and pepper.

5 Melt the butter in a large saucepan. Add the pasta and the parsley and stir briefly. Spoon the pasta into a serving dish. Remove the bay leaf and thyme sprig from the paprika sauce and serve with the pasta.

Step 1

Step 2

Step 4

Preparation: **20** Min Cooking: **25** Min
Per Serving: 465 kcal/1965 kJ;
12g protein; 13g fat;
97g carbohydrate

TYPICALLY HUNGARIAN

Paprika is made from a particular variety of red pepper. Available from mild to very hot, paprika powder is the most widely used spice in Hungarian cuisine as well as being an important export. It is cultivated mainly around Szeged and Kalocsa and called the 'red gold' of Hungary.

COOKING TIP

When roasting peppers, check them frequently so they char evenly. The skin is easier to peel off if the peppers are cooked then placed for 10–15 minutes under a damp tea-towel or in a sealed plastic bag. Roasting and skinning the peppers gives them a sweeter flavour and makes them easier to digest.

SERVING TIP

For a pretty and aromatic napkin ring, tie a small bundle of fresh mixed herbs to each guest's serviette.

A dry Hungarian Tokaji or any other tangy white wine with lots of bouquet is the best accompaniment to this dish.

PENNE AMERICAN-STYLE

USA

Tender broccoli florets and penne, flavoured with garlic and hot chillies, are popular all over the United States — from California to New England.

INGREDIENTS
(Serves 4)

- 400g/14oz penne
- salt and black pepper

FOR THE VEG MIXTURE
- 500g/1lb 2oz broccoli
- 2 cloves garlic
- 1-2 fresh red chillies
- 6 anchovy fillets, optional
- a little milk, optional
- 20g/¾oz pine nuts
- 4 tbsp olive oil

INGREDIENTS TIP

For this dish, the broccoli can be substituted with baby sweetcorn, cauliflower, courgettes, or young carrots. It's best to choose vegetables which are in season. The recipe also tastes delicious with peeled prawns, chopped turkey or chicken.

1 Trim the broccoli, cut into florets, halve the florets and wash well. Slice any thick stems. Blanch in boiling, salted water until just tender. Drain and rinse with cold water.

2 Peel the garlic and chop finely. Halve the chillies, discard the seeds and chop finely. Wash your hands thoroughly. Soak the anchovy fillets in the milk, if using; drain and cut into small pieces.

3 Cook the penne in a large saucepan of salted, boiling water until al dente (see packet instructions).

4 Meanwhile, heat a frying pan without adding any fat. Add the pine nuts and fry briefly until golden brown.

5 Remove the nuts from the frying pan. Heat the oil in the pan, add the garlic and chillies and fry gently. Add the broccoli and anchovies, if using and cook briefly. Season with salt and pepper.

6 Drain the penne well and add to the broccoli mixture. Carefully toss all the ingredients together. Sprinkle with the pine nuts and serve hot.

Step 1

Step 4

Step 5

Preparation: **10** Min Cooking: 15 Min
Per Serving: 608 kcal/2559 kJ;
23g protein; 25g fat;
78g carbohydrate

TYPICALLY AMERICAN
Broccoli, long a favourite in Italy, was almost unknown in America until the late 1920s when an enterprising Italian farmer in California began advertising his broccoli crop on the radio. It is now on large plantations, all over the American continent.

COOKING TIP

The Americans prepare traditional pasta dishes with little sauce. You can add fresh, diced tomatoes to make more liquid, but use fully ripe or canned tomatoes for a good flavour. Add the diced tomatoes to the pan at the same time as the broccoli.

SERVING TIP

Serve grated cheese, ideally a strong, mature pecorino, with this dish.

 Try a light American beer or alcohol-free lager to accompany this meal.

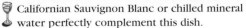 Californian Sauvignon Blanc or chilled mineral water perfectly complement this dish.

$\mathcal{F}$ARFALLE WITH COLOURFUL SPRING VEGETABLES

USA

The combination of tender asparagus, fresh mushrooms and mange tout makes this a delicious meal that's rich in vitamins. Adding a few dried mushrooms intensifies the flavour.

INGREDIENTS
(Serves 4)

- 400g/14oz farfalle
- salt

FOR THE VEGETABLE SAUCE
- 25g/1oz dried mushrooms
- 200g/7oz asparagus
- salt and black pepper
- slice of lemon
- 100g/4oz mushrooms
- 150g/5oz mange tout
- 1 young carrot
- 100g/4oz frozen peas
- 100g/4oz back bacon
- 3 tbsp olive oil
- 90ml/3fl oz dry white wine
- 200ml/7fl oz double cream
- pinch of oregano
- pinch of marjoram

INGREDIENTS TIP

Dried mushrooms are available from delicatessens and larger supermarkets.

1 Bring the dried mushrooms to the boil in 150ml/¼ pint water, set aside and leave to soak. Trim and wash the asparagus and peel the tough bottom third of the stalks. Add the lemon slice to a saucepan of salted water and bring to the boil. Add the asparagus and cook for 10–15 minutes, or until just tender. Drain the asparagus well.

2 Trim the fresh mushrooms and cut into quarters. Top and tail the mange tout, and cut into strips. Trim, peel and dice the carrot. Cook the mange tout, carrot and peas for 3 minutes in salted, boiling water. Drain well. Cut the bacon into strips.

3 Cook the farfalle in a large saucepan of salted, boiling water until al dente (see packet instructions) and drain well. Drain the dried mushrooms.

4 Heat the oil in a frying pan. Add the vegetables, dried mushrooms and bacon and cook for 2 minutes. Pour in the wine and cream. Stir well and cook until the sauce takes on a creamy consistency. Add salt, pepper and the herbs. Toss with the pasta, season with pepper and serve hot.

Step 1

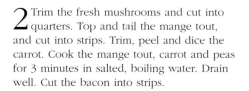

Step 2

Step 4

Preparation: **25** Min Cooking: **30** Min
Per Serving: 780 kcal/3280 kJ;
23g protein; 39g fat;
75g carbohydrate

TYPICALLY 'LITTLE ITALY'
When Italians emigrated to New York at the turn of the century, they brought the culinary habits of home to parts of the city. Centred around Manhattan's Lower East Side, the profusion of Italian restaurants and shops has caused the area to be renamed 'Little Italy'.

CALIFORNIAN SPAGHETTI TETRAZZINI

USA

This rich and delicious dish is dedicated to the great Italian soprano Louisa Tetrazzini. A delicate, creamy chicken sauce coats the pasta and the whole dish has a golden, cheesy finish.

INGREDIENTS
(Serves 4)

- 400g/14oz spaghetti
- salt
- 25g/1oz butter, diced
- 40g/1½oz grated cheese

FOR THE SAUCE

- 1 onion
- 25g/1oz butter
- 150ml/¼ pint white wine
- 500ml/18fl oz chicken stock
- 1 bay leaf
- 500g/1lb 2oz chicken breasts, skinned and boned
- 1 tbsp plain flour
- 142ml/5fl oz double cream
- salt and white pepper
- juice of ½ lemon
- 1 egg yolk

INGREDIENTS TIP

Fresh stock is now widely available and has a superior flavour to stock cubes.

1 For the sauce, peel the onion and chop finely. Melt half the butter in a pan and cook the onion until softened. Add the wine, pour in the stock and add the bay leaf.

2 Bring to the boil, add the chicken and reduce the heat. Cover and simmer for 10 minutes. Remove the chicken from the pan. Bring the cooking juices back to the boil, then strain and reserve the liquid. Cook the spaghetti in plenty of salted, boiling water until al dente (see packet instructions). Drain and rinse with cold water.

3 Melt the remaining butter for the sauce in a pan. Stir in the flour and gradually add the strained juices. Simmer for 10 minutes. Stir in the cream and cook until thickened. Season with salt, pepper and lemon juice. Remove from the heat. Preheat the oven to 180°C/350°F/Gas 4. Dice the chicken.

4 Transfer the spaghetti to a greased ovenproof dish. Add the chicken to the sauce and stir in the egg yolk. Make a shallow hollow in the spaghetti and pour in the sauce. Dot with the diced butter and sprinkle with cheese. Bake for 20 minutes, or until the top is browned and crispy.

Step 1

Step 3

Step 4

Preparation: **10** Min Cooking: **1** Hour
Per Serving: 842 kcal/3533 kJ;
44g protein; 39g fat;
78g carbohydrate

TYPICALLY CALIFORNIAN

San Francisco is a cosmopolitan city and is well known for its many restaurants serving dishes from all over the world, including Italian pasta. This unusual pasta dish was first created to celebrate the much acclaimed performance of a visiting diva – Louisa Tetrazzini – at the opera house.

COOKING TIP

In Step 3, a roux is made for the sauce. To keep the sauce creamy and smooth, melt the butter in the saucepan and gradually add the flour, off the heat, stirring all the time. Add the stock a little at a time, still off the heat, then simmer to cook the sauce.

SERVING TIP

As a dessert, serve real American ice-cream: fruit, vanilla or chocolate-flavour – whichever is your favourite.

 A dry Californian white wine is the ideal accompaniment to this dish.

45

PAPPARDELLE WITH HAM AUSTRALIAN-STYLE

AUSTRALIA

INGREDIENTS
(Serves 4)

- 400g/14oz pappardelle
- salt
- chives or sliced spring onion tops, to garnish

FOR THE SAUCE
- 125g/4½oz Parma ham
- 75g/3oz cooked ham
- 60g/2½oz butter
- 284ml/10fl oz pint double cream
- pinch of grated nutmeg
- white pepper
- 75g/3oz freshly grated Parmesan cheese

INGREDIENTS TIP
Instead of Parma ham, you can use any other mildly smoked ham or cooked bacon, or add cooked seasonal vegetables, such as broccoli or garden peas.

Pappardelle, the broadest variety of all ribbon pastas, is served tossed in a thick cream and cheese sauce. Parma ham gives the clue to the origins of the dish.

1 For the sauce, cut the Parma ham and the cooked ham into strips with a sharp knife, or scissors, then dice finely.

2 Melt the butter in a shallow saucepan and add the diced ham. Cook briefly, then add the cream and reduce the heat. Cook for 8–10 minutes, or until the sauce thickens and then season with the nutmeg and white pepper.

Step 1

3 Stir the Parmesan cheese into the sauce and simmer for a few minutes over a medium heat.

4 Meanwhile, cook the pappardelle in a large saucepan of salted, boiling water until al dente (see packet instructions). Chop the chives or spring onion tops finely.

Step 4

5 Drain the pappardelle in a large colander, then divide between four warmed plates or bowls. Pour the hot sauce over the top, sprinkle with the chopped chives or spring onion tops and serve hot.

Step 5

Preparation: **20** Min Cooking: **10** Min
Per Serving: 880 kcal/3700 kJ;
31g protein; 54g fat;
72g carbohydrate

TYPICALLY AUSTRALIAN
In the original Italian recipe, 'Pappardelle alla lepre', the sauce is prepared using hare rather than cooked ham. The Italian settlers who emigrated to Australia adapted the recipe to their new environment and the ingredients they had available in their adopted country.

COOKING TIP

Parma ham is quite salty, so add salt sparingly.
This dish is also delicious cooked au gratin — stir an
egg yolk into the sauce, add the pasta and spoon into
a shallow heatproof dish. Sprinkle with more grated
cheese then grill until the cheese melts.

SERVING TIP

A colourful seafood salad makes
an excellent starter.

Serve with an Australian white
wine from the famous Barossa Valley vineyards.

3 WAYS WITH CREAMY PASTA SAUCE

The classic Carbonara sauce is made with cheese, bacon and eggs and is a universal favourite. Here we introduce the Italian original plus new variations from Spain and the USA.

LINGUINE IN SEAFOOD CARBONARA

Preparation: **10** Min   Cooking: **15** Min

SPAIN

(SERVES 4)
- 400g/14oz linguine
- salt

FOR THE SAUCE
- 1 bunch spring onions
- 1 clove garlic
- 2 tbsp olive oil
- 200g/7oz peeled prawns
- salt and white pepper
- lemon juice
- 4 eggs

1 Cook the linguine in salted, boiling water until al dente (see packet instructions).

2 Trim and wash the spring onions and slice finely. Peel and finely chop the garlic clove.

3 Heat the oil, add the onions and the garlic and cook briefly. Add the prawns and cook for a couple of minutes to heat through. Season with salt, pepper and lemon juice.

4 Beat the eggs and season. Drain the linguine well and toss with the prawns. Add the eggs, toss with the pasta and serve hot.

FARFALLE I PAPRIKA

Preparation: **10** M

USA

(SERVES 4)
- 400g/14oz farfalle
- salt

FOR THE SAUCE
- 1 red and 1 green pepper
- 1 onion
- 2 tbsp olive oil
- 3 eggs
- salt and white pepper
- pinch of paprika powder

1 Cook the farfalle in salted, boiling water until al dente (see packet instructions). Cut the peppers in half, remove seeds and

GREEN SPAGHETTI IN CLASSIC CARBONARA

Preparation: **15** Min   Cooking: **15** Min

ITALY

(SERVES 4)
- 400g/14oz green spaghetti
- salt

FOR THE SAUCE
- 4 eggs
- 5 tbsp double cream
- 100g/4oz Parmesan
- salt and white pepper
- 250g/9oz streaky bacon
- 1 tbsp olive oil

1 Cook the spaghetti in salted, boiling water until al dente.

2 Beat the eggs with the cream in a large bowl. Grate the cheese and stir into the eggs. Season with plenty of salt and pepper.

3 Cut the rind off the bacon and dice finely. Heat the oil and fry the bacon, stirring frequently, until crispy.

4 Drain the spaghetti well. Add to the pan with the bacon and mix well.

5 Remove the pan from the heat. Pour the eggs and cream over the spaghetti and bacon mixture and toss quickly. Serve immediately.

ROMATIC ARBONARA

oking: **15** Min

white pith and cut into cubes. Peel and chop the onion.

2 Heat the oil in a frying pan. Add the diced peppers and onion and cook until softened but not browned.

3 Beat the eggs thoroughly with the salt, pepper and paprika powder.

4 Drain the farfalle well. Add the pasta to the frying pan and mix well with the pepper and onion mixture. Pour in the eggs, quickly toss with the farfalle and serve immediately.

 SERVING TIP Serve extra soy sauce separately, for guests who like its strong, salty flavour.

Chinese jasmine tea is a refreshing drink that suits these eastern flavours.

$\mathcal{S}$INGAPORE NOODLES WITH PRAWNS

SINGAPORE

Ginger, garlic and hot chilli give an exotic, unmistakably Singaporean touch to the golden Chinese egg noodles, crunchy vegetables and succulent prawns.

INGREDIENTS
(Serves 4)

- 250g/9oz egg noodles
- salt and black pepper

FOR THE STIR-FRY
- 150g/5oz carrots
- 2 spring onions
- 1 yellow pepper
- 1 clove garlic
- 2 chillies
- 2.5cm/1in fresh root ginger
- 200g/7oz peeled and cooked prawns
- 3 tbsp vegetable oil
- 150g/5oz beansprouts
- 5 tbsp soy sauce

INGREDIENTS TIP

Briefly rinse the beansprouts in cold water before cooking them, then pat dry on kitchen paper to stop them turning soggy. To vary the vegetables, try adding baby sweetcorn or bamboo shoots.

1 Cook the egg noodles in plenty of salted, boiling water (see packet instructions). Drain the noodles well in a colander.

2 Trim and wash the vegetables. Cut the carrots into fine strips. Slice the spring onions finely. De-seed the pepper and dice.

3 Peel the garlic and chop finely. Halve the chillies, remove the seeds and chop the flesh finely. Wash your hands thoroughly. Peel the ginger and cut into fine strips. Wash the prawns and pat dry on kitchen paper.

4 Heat the oil in a wok over a medium heat. When it is hot, add the garlic, chillies and ginger. Fry, stirring, for 1 minute, then add the vegetables and beansprouts and stir-fry for 5 minutes.

5 Add the egg noodles, stir in the prawns and toss together with the vegetables for 1–2 minutes to heat through. Season with salt, pepper and the soy sauce. Mix all the ingredients together, coating the noodles with the sauce, and serve immediately.

Step 1

Step 3

Step 5

Preparation **20** Min Cooking **15** Min
Per Serving: 470 kcal/1973 kJ;
24g protein; 19g fat;
55g carbohydrate

TYPICALLY SINGAPORE
With its large busy harbour, Singapore is a centre of international trade. The famous night market is regarded as a gourmet's paradise where exotic delicacies from all around the world, such as shark's fin and snake meat, can be sampled.

JAPANESE RICE NOODLES WITH MUSHROOMS

JAPAN

This simple vegetarian noodle dish comes from the land of the cherry blossom. It's quick and easy to prepare yet exudes charm and sophistication.

INGREDIENTS
(Serves 4)

FOR THE NOODLES
- 2 eggs
- 1 egg yolk
- 1 tbsp vegetable oil
- 1 tsp salt
- 150g/5oz Japanese rice flour
- 100g/4oz plain flour

FOR THE SAUCE
- 400g/14oz fresh shiitake mushrooms
- 20 cherry tomatoes
- 50g/2oz butter
- salt and black pepper
- 2 tbsp double cream
- juice of 1 lime
- fresh basil sprigs

INGREDIENTS TIP

Making your own noodles is fun but also time-consuming so buy ready-made oriental rice noodles if you prefer. Cook them according to the packet instructions.

1 For the noodles, place the eggs and the egg yolk in a bowl. Add the oil and salt and beat together. Gradually sieve the rice flour and plain flour onto the eggs. Work the ingredients together and knead to make a smooth dough, adding a little water if necessary. The dough is ready when it is smooth and the side of the bowl is clean. Leave the dough to rest for 20 minutes.

Step 1

2 For the sauce, place the mushrooms in a colander and rinse thoroughly with cold water. Cut into slices. Wash the tomatoes.

3 For the noodles, roll out the dough into a thin sheet and cut into strands 6mm/¹⁄₄in wide. Cook the noodles in a large saucepan of salted, boiling water for 2–3 minutes until al dente. Drain well.

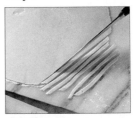
Step 3

4 Melt the butter in a frying pan, add the mushrooms and cook briefly. Season with salt and pepper. Add the tomatoes, then the noodles. Pour in the cream and lime juice and mix all the ingredients well.

5 Arrange the rice noodles, mushroom and vegetable mixture in small bowls and garnish with basil sprigs.

Step 4

Preparation: **30** Min (plus resting)
Cooking: **10** Min
Per Serving: 446 kcal/1946 kJ;
11g protein; 23g fat;
53g carbohydrate

TYPICALLY JAPANESE
Rice is the staple food of the Japanese and is served at any time of day. It is the most important ingredient of sake, the Japanese rice wine, and was considered a sign of wealth in former times. Rice flour is used to make Japanese rice and cellophane noodles.

COOKING TIP

Use fresh shiitake mushrooms, if possible, as their flavour is more delicate than dried – you should be able to find them in most larger supermarkets amongst the vegetables. Oyster or chestnut mushrooms can be used as an alternative.

SERVING TIP

Use decorative lacquer bowls and matching chopsticks for a fun Japanese meal with friends.

 The traditional Japanese drink is sake, but a light beer also goes well with these noodles.

WOK NOODLES WITH PORK

CHINA

INGREDIENTS
(Serves 4)

- 450g/1lb pork fillet
- bunch of spring onions
- 1 clove garlic
- 200g/7oz egg noodles
- salt
- 150ml/¼ pint vegetable oil

FOR THE MARINADE
- pinch of ground ginger
- salt and pepper
- 1 tbsp soy sauce
- 1 tbsp oyster sauce
- 1 tbsp sesame oil

FOR THE SAUCE
- 1 tsp sugar
- 1 tsp soy sauce
- 1 tsp oyster sauce
- 1 tsp sesame oil
- 1 tbsp cornflour
- 125ml/4fl oz chicken stock

INGREDIENTS TIP

The oyster sauce can be substituted with extra soy sauce if you prefer.

Piquant marinated pork and spring onions tossed with crispy fried egg noodles and combined with aromatic sesame oil and rich soy sauce makes a stylish Chinese feast.

1 Mix all the ingredients for the marinade together in a bowl. Cut the pork into thin strips, toss in the marinade and leave to stand for 30 minutes.

2 Trim the spring onions, cut into pieces 3cm/1¼in long, then halve lengthways if preferred. Peel the garlic and chop finely. Mix together all the ingredients for the sauce in a small bowl.

Step 1

3 Cook the noodles in plenty of salted, boiling water until al dente. Pour into a colander, rinse with cold water and drain well. Heat the vegetable oil in a wok until fairly hot. Fry the noodles until crispy and golden brown and set aside.

Step 2

4 Drain all but 2 tablespoons of oil from the wok. Add the garlic, cook briefly, then add the pork and cook for 2–3 minutes, stirring continuously. Add the spring onions and stir in the sauce. As soon as the liquid starts to thicken, stir well and remove the wok from the heat.

Step 3

5 Arrange the egg noodles on a serving dish and spoon the pork mixture into the centre. Serve immediately.

Preparation: **15** Min
Marinating: **30** Min
Cooking: **10** Min

Per Serving: 670 kcal/2815 kJ;
19g protein; 55g fat;
28g carbohydrate

TYPICALLY CHINESE

The wok is the most important cooking pot in China. In former times, it was used for cooking over an open fire – this explains its rounded base which ensures even heat distribution. As well as woks, the Chinese also use bamboo steamers for cooking.

COOKING TIPS

If you do not own a wok, use a large cast iron frying pan for frying the noodles as it conducts the heat evenly and stays hot for a long time • For a more spicy dish, try adding Sichuan black pepper to the pork mixture at the end of Step 4.

SERVING TIP

The Chinese serve this dish with a salad of grated bamboo shoots, beansprouts and Chinese cabbage.

 Green tea is the oriental choice, or try a light rosé wine from Provence.

VERMICELLI WITH PRAWNS

CHINA

Crispy fried vermicelli topped with a sumptuous mixture of tender vegetables and juicy prawns flavoured with garlic and ginger, brings a taste of China to the table.

INGREDIENTS
(Serves 4)

- 15g/½oz dried Chinese mushrooms
- 1 clove garlic
- 2cm/¾in fresh ginger root
- 2 spring onions
- 2 carrots
- 100g/4oz mange tout
- 250g/9oz uncooked prawns
- 175g/6oz Chinese vermicelli
- 6 tbsp vegetable oil
- salt and black pepper
- five spice powder
- 50g/2oz cashew nuts
- 125ml/4fl oz chicken or vegetable stock
- 2 tbsp oyster sauce

INGREDIENTS TIP

Dried oriental mushrooms add their own distinct flavour so are worth tracking down in shops specialising in oriental or Chinese foods.

1 Put the dried mushrooms in a large bowl, cover with boiling water and leave to stand for 1 hour. Peel and chop the garlic and peel and dice the ginger. Trim, wash and slice the vegetables. Peel the prawns, cut a slit along the back and remove the dark thread.

2 Cook the vermicelli in plenty of salted, boiling water until al dente. Drain, spread on kitchen paper and pat dry.

3 Heat 2 tablespoons of oil in a wok, add the garlic and ginger and stir-fry until softened. Add the prawns and stir-fry until they turn pink. Remove from the wok and add 2 tablespoons of oil. Stir-fry the vegetables for 5 minutes. Season with salt, pepper and five spice powder.

4 Drain the mushrooms, cut into quarters, and add to the wok with the nuts. Pour in the stock and the oyster sauce. Stir in the prawns and simmer for 2 minutes. Remove the mixture from the wok and keep warm.

5 Heat the remaining oil in the wok and stir-fry the vermicelli until golden brown. Top with the vegetable mix and serve.

Step 1

Step 1

Step 4

Preparation: **20** Min
Standing: **1** Hour
Cooking: **10** Min
Per Serving: 541 kcal/2268 kJ;
24g protein; 29g fat;
44g carbohydrate

TYPICALLY CHINESE

Seasoning is of vital importance in oriental cooking. Chinese market stalls sag under the weight of a dazzling choice of spices and flavourings. Amongst the most common ingredients are ginger, garlic and spring onions, which are used in many dishes.

COOKING TIPS

When cooking the vermicelli follow the packet instructions carefully as most oriental noodles need less cooking time than Italian pasta – often just a few minutes in boiling water • The sweetish, piquant aroma and flavour of oyster sauce can be quite dominant so use sparingly, if you prefer.

SERVING TIP

For a simple, refreshing dessert, serve fresh lychees and garnish with mint.

 In China, a festive meal like this would be served with tea and rice wine but a spritzer — white wine with fizzy water is perfect for western tastes.

57

SHANGHAI NOODLES WITH CHICKEN

CHINA

This combination of fine egg noodles with a stir-fry of chicken, pak choi and sesame seeds is typical of the dishes from the busy seaport metropolis of Shanghai on China's east coast.

INGREDIENTS
(Serves 4)

- 275g/10oz chicken breasts, skinned and boned
- 500g/1lb 2oz pak choi
- 2 cloves garlic
- 250g/9oz egg noodles
- 1 tsp sesame seeds
- 3 tbsp vegetable oil
- salt and black pepper
- 2 tbsp soy sauce
- 1 tsp cornflour
- 1 tsp sesame oil

INGREDIENTS TIP

Pak choi (or bok choy) is a slightly bitter-tasting variety of cabbage often used in stir-fried dishes. You may use white cabbage or Chinese leaves instead. If you do, season the dish more generously.

1 Wash the chicken breasts, pat dry and cut into small pieces. Cut the pak choi in half, remove the stalk and shred the leaves. Peel the garlic and chop finely.

2 Cook the egg noodles in a large saucepan of salted, boiling water until al dente (see packet instructions). Pour into a colander and drain well.

3 Heat a wok, or large frying pan, add the sesame seeds and toast lightly. Pour in the oil and fry the garlic briefly. Add the chicken pieces and stir-fry over a high heat, for 2–3 minutes. Season with salt and pepper and push to the edge of the wok. Add the pak choi and cook until al dente, stirring continuously. Stir in the soy sauce.

4 Toss all the ingredients in the wok together well. Blend the cornflour with a little water and pour into the wok. Stir until the pan juices have thickened a little. Remove from the heat.

5 Add the sesame oil and noodles to the wok and mix well. Serve in small bowls or soup plates.

Step 1

Step 4

Step 5

Preparation: **15** Min Cooking: **15** Min
Per Serving: 479 kcal/2012 kJ;
24g protein; 22g fat;
49g carbohydrate

TYPICALLY SHANGHI

The cuisine of Shanghai is arguably China's finest, boasting a delicious choice of chicken dishes — slowly stewed, steamed or stir-fried — with a wide range of fresh vegetables and spices. The port is also famous for its fresh fish and seafood.

COOKING TIP

Sesame seeds fully develop their aroma when toasted without oil. Sesame oil has a strong, nutty aroma. Do not allow it to boil as this further intensifies its flavour, which will then overwhelm the other ingredients.

SERVING TIP

Serve clear chicken broth with vegetable strips as a starter.

 Serve with chilled still or sparkling mineral water or iced lager.

CLASSIC INDONESIAN NOODLES

INDONESIA

Crispy fried egg noodles form the basis of Indonesia's national dish. Here they are prepared using chicken breast, pork, prawns and a variety of seasonal vegetables.

INGREDIENTS
(Serves 4)

- 250g/9oz egg noodles
- salt
- chervil or coriander leaves, to garnish

FOR THE STIR-FRY
- 2 spring onions
- 150g/5oz Chinese leaves
- 2 chillies
- 1 onion
- 3 cloves garlic
- 1cm/½in fresh ginger root
- 200g/7oz chicken breast
- 200g/7oz pork fillet
- 100ml/3½fl oz vegetable oil
- 150g/5oz beansprouts
- 100g/4oz cooked prawns
- pinch of sugar
- 2 tbsp soy sauce

INGREDIENTS TIP

Instead of Chinese leaves, use the finer cabbage, pak choi (bok choy) or fresh spinach.

1 Place the egg noodles in a large saucepan of salted, boiling water and separate with a fork. Cook the noodles until al dente (see packet instructions). Pour into a colander, rinse under cold water and drain well.

2 Wash the spring onions and Chinese leaves and shred finely. Cut the chillies in half, remove the seeds and chop finely. Peel the onion, garlic and ginger and chop finely. Cut the chicken and pork into strips.

3 Heat the oil in a wok, add the noodles and fry until crispy. Remove the noodles from the wok and set aside.

4 Drain off all but 2 tablespoons of oil. Add the chicken, pork, chillies, onion, garlic and ginger and stir-fry for 4–5 minutes. Add the beansprouts with the remaining vegetables and stir-fry for 2–3 minutes. Stir in the prawns, sugar and soy sauce and toss together for 1–2 minutes.

5 Return the egg noodles to the wok and toss all the ingredients thoroughly. Arrange on individual plates and serve garnished with chervil or coriander leaves.

Step 2

Step 3

Step 4

Preparation: **25** Min Cooking: 20 Min
Per Serving: 829 kcal/3491 kJ;
32g protein; 31g fat;
112g carbohydrate

TYPICALLY INDONESIAN
The Republic of Indonesia consists of over 13,000 islands, including Borneo, Bali, Sumatra and Java and every region produces its own variation of national dishes. Probably the best known dish is Nasi Goreng, a baked rice dish. Bami Goreng, the Indonesian name for the recipe here is its stir-fried counterpart.

COOKING TIPS

If you do not own a wok, you can cook this dish in a large, deep frying pan instead • Fresh ginger, peeled, sliced and stored in groundnut oil, can be kept for several months • Use frozen prawns if you prefer but allow them to defrost first.

SERVING TIP

Serve this dish with crisp prawn crackers or with pancakes, rolled and sliced into rounds.

Choose a light red wine such as Valpolicella, or jasmine tea, to accompany this dish.

DICTIONARY OF TERMS

An understanding of the following terms and ingredients is useful when cooking pasta and noodle dishes.

Al Dente is an expression used when cooking pasta. It means that the pasta should still be slightly chewy and should not be soft and soggy. Cooking times vary depending on the type of pasta used. Always check the packet instructions and test the pasta regularly during cooking.

Balsamic vinegar is distilled from wine. Matured for at least 15 years in wood it has a strong concentrated flavour. It is produced in north Italy, where it is known as aceto balsamico. It is often used in salad dressings.

Basil is a herb used extensively in Mediterranean cooking. It has a slightly sweet, peppery taste and a distinct aroma. Apart from the popular green variety, there are a number of purple varieties, with crinkled leaves, as well as the red 'dark opal' basil. Basil goes well with tomato, egg and fish dishes, soups and risottos. Shred the leaves rather than chopping them and add to dishes at the last minute to retain flavour.

Chinese Leaf is an oriental cabbage with tightly packed, crisp, green leaves. This versatile vegetable is used in China for soups, or stir-fried with meat. Its mild taste means it goes well with richly flavoured ingredients.

Five Spice Powder is a finely ground mixture of star anise, fennel, cinnamon, cloves and Sichuan peppercorns. It is used in a wide range of oriental dishes for its pungent, spicy, slightly sweet flavour.

Oregano is a herb with a pungent taste and aroma. It is often used in Mediterranean cooking to add flavour to tomato dishes and sauces.

Oyster Sauce is a thick, brown, rich sauce and a popular seasoning from southern China. Made from a concentrated blend of oysters cooked in soy sauce and seasonings, it has a rich, but not fishy flavour. As well as being used for cooking, it makes a good dipping sauce for meat or vegetables, diluted with a little oil.

Parma Ham or prosciutto is a classic Italian ham. It comes from pigs fed on the whey left over from producing the local cheese — Parmesan. The ham is dry-cured under weights to flatten it, then left to mature. It is usually sold very thinly sliced in packets and can be served raw or lightly cooked.

TYPES OF OLIVE OIL

Olive oil is extracted from the flesh and stones of olives. Its distinctive flavour depends on the type of olive, the year of harvest, the climate and soil. Quality varies, depending on how the oil is produced.

EXTRA VIRGIN OLIVE OIL
Unrefined oil from the first pressing of the olives, produced without heat or chemicals. It is the best tasting and best quality oil. Also called 'cold-pressed extra virgin olive oil'.

VIRGIN OLIVE OIL
Pure olive oil after the second pressing where the olives are heated. The oil is purified and filtered but not refined.

PURE OLIVE OIL
A blend of extra virgin and refined olive oil. This is a basic and less expensive oil, good for everyday cooking.

Parmesan is a piquant Italian hard cheese. It is made from cows' milk according to strict regulations around the rivers Po and Reno in northern Italy. It is usually served, freshly grated, with Italian pasta dishes and risottos, but it is also used in salads, to make pesto sauce and as a filling for ravioli. Parmigiano Reggiano is the finest quality Parmesan.

Pecorino cheese is produced in central and southern Italy and is made from sheeps' milk. It is sold fresh or matured. The more mature varieties include pecorino Romano (from the Lazio region) and pecorino Sardo (from Sardinia), the latter being stronger in taste.

Pesto is a classic Italian sauce made from basil, Parmesan, garlic and pine nuts. Along the Ligurian coast, pesto is particularly popular as a pasta sauce – it is available in many blends made with a variety of different ingredients.

Pine Nuts, or kernels, are the seeds from pine cones. In Italy they are mainly used ground in pesto sauce, but are also found in desserts and biscuits. Toasting them lightly in a dry, non-greased frying pan before using intensifies their flavour.

TYPES OF NOODLES

CELLOPHANE NOODLES
Also called transparent or bean thread noodles, they are made from mung beans. The noodles are soaked in hot water, not boiled, and are then drained and added to soups or braised dishes. They can also be deep-fried and used as a garnish.

CHINESE EGG NOODLES
Spaghetti-like noodles made from wheat flour and eggs. In Asian cooking, egg noodles are often added to soups or stir-fried in a wok and served with meats, prawns and vegetables.

RICE NOODLES
Rice noodles are most popular in southern China. Fresh rice noodles are only sold in oriental grocers but dried varieties are more widely available. The dried noodles are soaked in warm water until soft, then added to soups and stir-fries.

SOMEN (VERMICELLI)
Very thin, long noodles made from wheat flour and eggs. In Asia, these noodles are also produced from soy beans. They are added to soups to give bulk.

WHEAT NOODLES
Made from wheat flour, these noodles are similar to egg noodles, but paler in colour. They can be added to stir-fries and soups, or served as a side dish instead of rice.

Porcini, also known as ceps, are Italian wild mushrooms with deep rich flavour. When cooked they have a soft texture with just a little bite. Mainly sold dried, porcini are soaked in water before cooking and are used in small quantities in sauces, ragoûts and soups.

Ricotta is a white, creamy, Italian soft cheese, traditionally made from sheeps' milk, which is boiled twice. Today it is mainly produced from cows' milk. Ricotta is used frequently in Italian cooking, often as a filling in pastas such as cannelloni and ravioli, or in sweet desserts, such as cheesecakes.

Sage is a strongly aromatic herb with furry green leaves and a slightly bitter taste. It often flavours pork and veal.

Soy Sauce, an essential ingredient in Chinese cooking, is a popular sauce made from soya beans, flour and water. It is used to flavour stir-fries and noodle dishes or served on the side for dipping.

INDEX

Acknowledgements

Picture Credits
All cover and recipe pictures:
© International Masters Publishers BV.
Food Photography: Eising, Dorothee Gödert, Peter Rees, Manuel Schnell,
Neil Mersh, Philip Wilkins
Agency pictures:
Introduction: Look: Heeb, page 5 top left; Tony Stone: Allison, page 4, bottom
right; DeVore, page 5 bottom right, Huber, page 4/5 bottom middle
Pictures for the Typically sections: Anthony Blake: page 8, 26, 28, 32, 37, 39,
46, 51; Food Features: page 30
Cephas: Blythe, page 13; Kielty, page 45; Rock, page 57
Comstock: page 14
Garden Picture Library: Viard, page 58; Lamontagne, page 52
Robert Harding: page 23; Frerck, page 36,
Hutchison: Egan, page 38
Food Matters: Eriksson, page 20
Impact: Cormack, page 40; Edwards, page 6; Fear, page 18
Harry Smith Collection: page 11

Measuring Ingredients
Tsp – teaspoon, Tbsp – tablespoon
Teaspoons and tablespoons are level and measured using standard
measuring spoons.
Follow either metric or imperial measurements and don't mix the two.

Tony Stone: page 44; Sitton, page 52;
Telegraph Colour Library: Moss, page 58; The Stock Directory, page 56
With special thanks to David Mellor for supplying props
© International Masters Publishers BV
International Masters Publishers Ltd MCMXCVIII/MM
Reproduced by Studio One Origination, London, UK
Printed in Italy by Mondadori